J 004

D

DI

J 004

D

Play With Computers

Jim Drake

Heinemann Library
Des Plaines, Illinois

Designed by Visual Image
Printed in Hong Kong

03 02 01 00 99
10 9 8 7 6 5 4 3 2 1

Library of Congress Cataloging-in-Publication Data

Drake, Jim, 1955-
    Play with computers   / Jim Drake.
        p. cm. – (Log on to computers)
    Includes bibliographical references and index.
    Summary: A brief introduction to how computers are used as a means
 of entertainment, describing game software, animation, simulators,
 computer music, and the World Wide Web.
    ISBN 1-57572-786-2 (lib bdg.)
    1. Computers—Juvenile literature. [1. Computers.] I. Title.
 II. Series: Drake, Jim, 1955- Log on to computers.
    QA76.23.D73   1999
    004—dc21   98-48088
                                                          CIP
                                                           AC

Acknowledgments
The author and publishers would like to thank the following for permission to reproduce photographs: Trevor Clifford, pp. 4, 6, 7, 8, 14, 20, 24, 26; CYBERMIND UK Ltd, pp. 9, 12; Kobal Collection/Digital Domain. p. 19; Network/M. Goldwater, p. 10; PIct One Design Studio/Encyclopedia Britannica, pp. 22, 23; Powerstock, p. 25; Retna/Corlouer, p. 19; Science Photo Library/Gable/Jerrican, p. 28, J. King-Holmes, p. 11, J. King-Holmes/W. Industries, p. 13, S. Ogden, p. 5; Sygma, pp. 15, 19.

Illustrations on pages 16 and 17 by Ron Kamen.

Cover illustration by Andy Parker.

Every effort has been made to contact copyright holders of any material reproduced in this book. Any omissions will be rectified in subsequent printings if notice is given to the publisher.

Some words are shown in bold, **like this.** You can find out what they mean by looking in the glossary.

CONTENTS

WHAT CAN COMPUTERS DO?

A computer has to be told what to do. The instructions people give it are called **programs**. Another name for computer programs is **software**. Different programs help people to work, learn, and play. This book is about some of the ways that computer software can help us to have fun.

In the 1970s, computer games were very simple. People were excited because they had never seen anything like them.

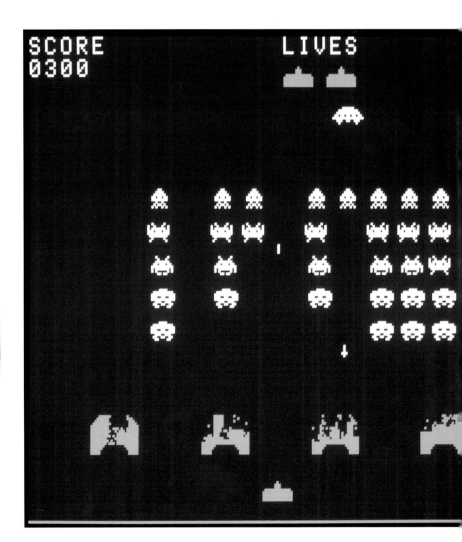

Computers help people talk to other people. They also help us to make pictures and sounds. As computers get more powerful, the pictures and sounds become much more realistic. With **virtual reality**, you can even feel as if you are inside a computer "world."

Many games today are very realistic. This game is almost like real skiing, but you don't get cold!

GAMES SOFTWARE

A computer game is one kind of **software**. Some games help people learn how to solve problems. Others can teach new skills. Many are just fun to play. An arcade game is a computer with only one kind of software. This means that you can only play one game on it. Games **consoles** and **PCs** let you play many different games.

You can play a hand-held computer game anywhere.

Computer game software comes in different forms. You can buy games software on **CD-ROMs**, disks, and cartridges. When you finish one game you can load a different one.

Each of these contains the program for a game.

GAMES CONSOLES

Games **consoles** like Sega™, Nintendo™, and Playstation™ are computers. They are made specially for playing games. They plug into a TV set. They don't need a keyboard. Usually they use gamepads. These are small and easy to hold in your hand. The best consoles may have three or more **microprocessors**.

This computer only plays games. The gamepads have buttons for moving around the screen and doing special commands.

8

Each microprocessor is like a separate computer. Each has a special job to do. One draws pictures on the screen. Another makes sounds. The most important microprocessor tells the others what to do. This makes games very realistic.

Some games make you think. Others test your skill using the gamepad.

SIMULATIONS

Some computer games are like things that people do in real life. These are called simulations. You can pretend to drive a car or fly a plane. Some simulators in arcades have moving seats to feel like the real thing. But not all simulations are just fun.

In a simulation, you can do things that you couldn't do in real life.

Aircraft pilots use simulations in training. They can practice takeoffs and landings. They can even practice what to do in an emergency. Weather **forecasters** use simulations. Reports from weather stations are used by a computer to figure out how the weather will change. But no simulation works exactly like the real thing!

To practice flying a real airplane costs a lot of money, especially if something goes wrong. Pilots can practice in a simulator until they are good enough to do the real thing.

VIRTUAL REALITY

This picture was taken through a virtual reality visor. As the person wearing the visor moves, the scene changes.

Most computers only have one screen. Pictures on a screen look flat. In real life, you see a slightly different picture with each eye. A **virtual reality visor** has two small screens. Each eye sees one screen. When the pictures are slightly different you think you see a picture that looks real, not flat.

Software changes the pictures so that you seem to be moving around inside the scene. A very powerful computer is needed to make the scene look real. You can use **virtual reality** to "see" places that you can't visit in real life.

This person sees a realistic view with the virtual reality visor. **With the special glove, he can feel things that aren't really there.**

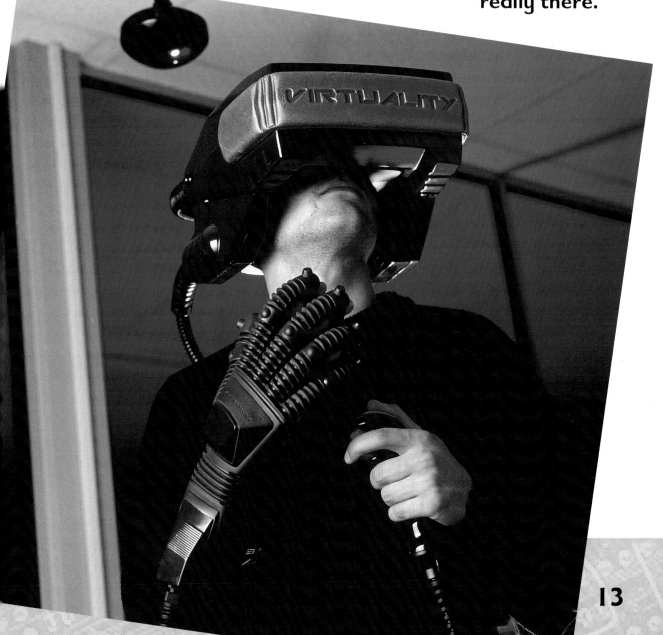

COMPUTER GRAPHICS

From close up, you can see the pixels on a screen. When you look from farther back, you can see the picture clearly.

Graphics is another word for pictures. Pictures on a computer screen are patterns of tiny dots. Each dot is called a pixel. If you look very carefully, you can see the pixels. The more pixels there are on the screen, the clearer the picture is. If you change the pixels, the picture changes. Computers can change the pixels very quickly.

Digital cameras and **scanners** turn pictures and photos into pixels. When a picture is on the screen, computer **programs** change the picture. Drawing and painting programs help make new pictures. Pictures can also be changed to make **special effects**.

Computers can change pictures on the screen. Strange faces can be created that would never be seen in real life.

15

ANIMATION

Cartoons are pictures that seem to move. Each second of cartoon film is made of 25 pictures, called frames. Each frame is slightly different from the one before it. When the frames are shown quickly, one after another, it looks as if you are seeing smooth movement. Another name for this is **animation**.

It takes a long time to draw all these pictures. Computers can help. They can figure out what the next picture should be. Computers make animations much more quickly than an artist. Computer animation is now used in many movies.

In one minute of a cartoon, there are over one thousand different pictures. This takes more than 150 feet (50 meters) of film.

ANIMATION IN MOVIES

Computers drew nearly 200 thousand film frames, like this, to make *Toy Story*.

Computers can **animate** pictures that would take too long to draw. *Toy Story* was the first full-length movie made using computer animation. Artists used computers to draw some of the pictures and the computers drew the rest. Earlier movies, like *Beauty and the Beast,* used some computer animation.

Many movies use computer animation for **special effects**. Many of the shipwreck scenes in the movie *Titanic* are computer animations. It is very expensive to build big film sets. Computer animation means a movie is cheaper to make.

Computer animation can show scenes that would be dangerous, difficult, or too expensive to film with real people.

MAKING MUSIC

Computers are now used to make music. Games **consoles** and most **PCs** have **sound cards**. A special **program** tells the card to make sounds. A **CD-ROM** drive can play music CDs. Some programs can help you practice playing an instrument.

These parts let a computer make music.

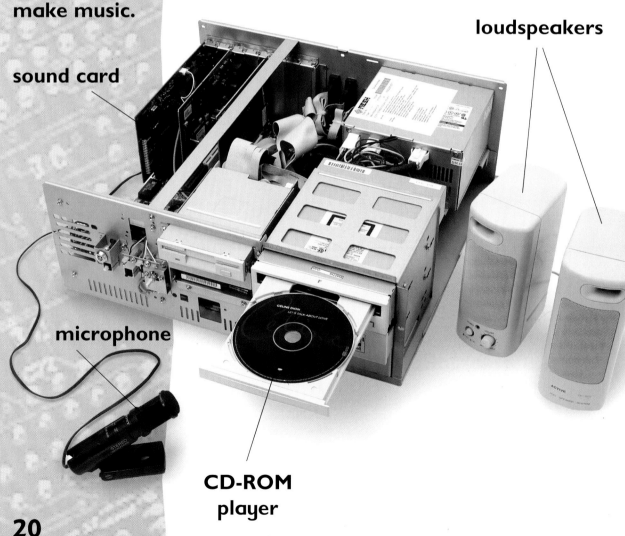

loudspeakers

sound card

microphone

CD-ROM player

Much modern music is made with the help of computers. Electronic instruments, like keyboards, can plug in to a computer. The computer tells the instruments the notes to play. Computer-controlled drum machines can make whatever beat they are programed to produce.

Computers can take the place of musicians. But people still need to write the programs.

CD-ROMS

CD-ROMs look just like music CDs. The shiny side holds **programs** or information. One CD-ROM can hold as many words as hundreds of books. Pictures, videos, and sounds can be put on a CD-Rom, too. Newer Digital Versatile Disks, called **DVDs,** look similar but can store about 30 times more information as a CD-ROM. DVDs may replace videotapes one day.

Computers can search very quickly for information. This could be a picture, a song, or a part from a video. One problem with CD-ROMs and DVDs is that, unlike books, you need a computer to read them.

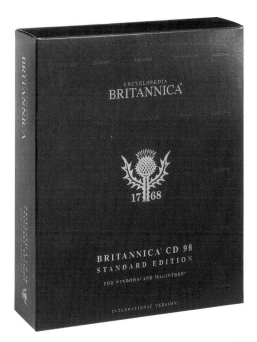

The 32 books of
this encyclopedia
have been put
on to one
CD-ROM.

COMPUTERS AND COMMUNICATION

A modem lets one computer connect to millions of other computers. You can see pictures and hear sounds from all over the world.

Computers help people communicate with other people. A **modem** lets a computer send messages through telephone lines. Other computers can read the message. This is called **e-mail.** People can send letters to friends this way. They can send pictures and sounds, too, using a camera and a microphone connected to the computer.

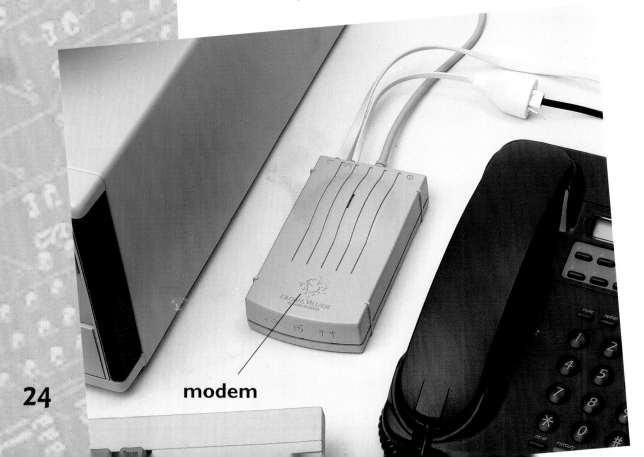

modem

The **Internet** connects computers all over the world. The World Wide Web is part of the Internet. You can use it to learn about your favorite singer or even to hear music and see moving pictures.

People in different countries can see each other and talk to each other by videoconferencing. Each person needs a computer with a video camera connected to it.

FUN ON THE INTERNET

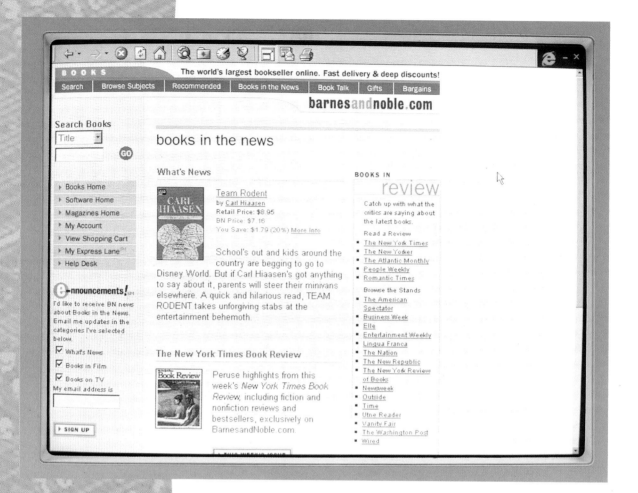

One way of buying books is by using a computer. The bookstore could be anywhere in the world.

People can buy many things without leaving home. One of the biggest bookstores in the world is called amazon.com. People cannot go in and buy a book. They must visit it on the **Internet** using a computer. When a person has decided what to buy, he or she pays electronically with a credit card. The books are delivered in the mail.

Many other things are sold in the same way. People can buy movie tickets or airplane tickets on the Internet. Two or more people can play the same game on their own computers, connected together through the Internet.

You can play this computer game with someone in a different town, or even in a different country.

THE FUTURE

Twenty years ago, no one imagined some of the things that computers can do today. In the future, there will be other uses for computers. Perhaps you will invent some of them!

You can get information from all over the world by using the Internet.

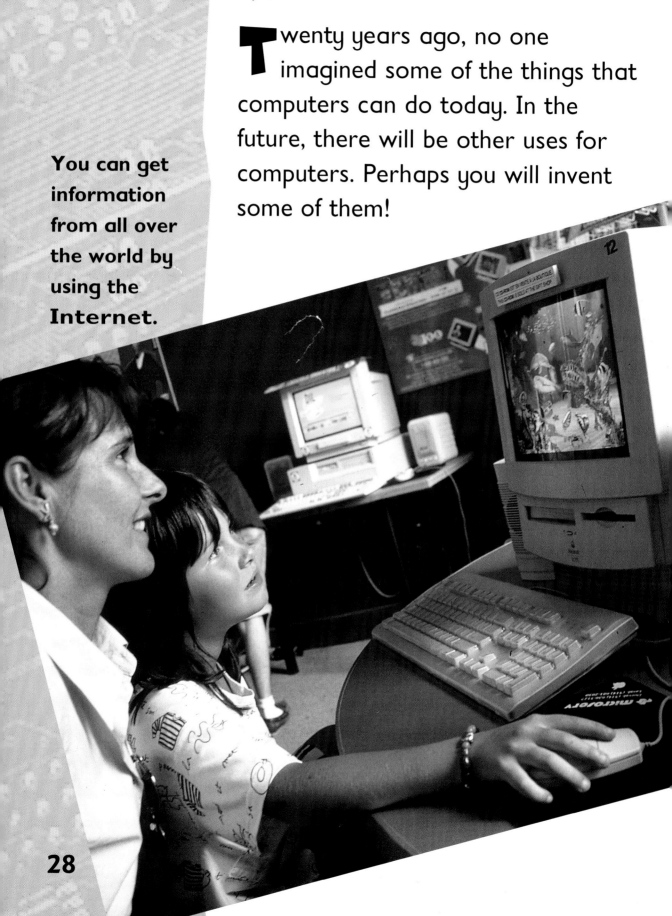

In your lifetime, computers will become smaller, faster, and more powerful. Perhaps computers will do all your work for you.

Some games are more fun to play outdoors with your friends.

GLOSSARY

animation many slightly different pictures, that when shown one after another very quickly, look like smooth movement

CD-ROM shiny disc that holds words, pictures, and music

console computer that plugs into a TV for playing games

digital camera camera that turns pictures into computer codes instead of using regular camera film

DVD (Digital Versatile Disk) disk like a CD-ROM, but that can hold much more information

e-mail electronic mail messages sent between computers

forecaster person who tries to predict what the weather will be

Internet network of computers around the world through which information is shared

microprocessor computer part that is the "brain" of a computer

modem machine that turns computer codes into sounds that can be sent through telephone lines

PC (Personal Computer) computers that are small enough to sit on a desk

program instructions that tell a computer what to do—also called software

scanner machine that turns pictures on paper into computer code

sound card computer part that allows a computer to play music and make other sounds

special effects strange or unusual sounds and pictures used in movies or television shows

virtual reality computer-created "world" where sights and sounds seem real and the user can interact

virtual reality visor special helmet with a computer screen in front of each eye

INDEX

MORE BOOKS TO READ

Brimmer, Larry D. *E-Mail*. Danbury, Conn: Children's Press, 1997.

Erlbach, Arlene. *Video Games*. Minneapolis Minn: Lerner Publishing Group, 1996.

Vander Hook, Sue. *Internet*. Mankato, Minn: Smart Apple Media, 1999.